Lightning
BOLT
BOOKS ™

Why Doesn't Everyone Eat Meat?

Vegetarianism and Special Diets

Jennifer Boothroyd

Lerner Publications • Minneapolis

For Mr. Kevin Spencer

Lerner Publications Company
A division of Lerner Publishing Group, Inc.
241 First Avenue North
Minneapolis, MN 55401 USA

For reading levels and more information, look up this title at www.lernerbooks.com.

Library of Congress Cataloging-in-Publication Data

Boothroyd, Jennifer, 1972- author.
    Why doesn't everyone eat meat? : vegetarianism and special diets / Jennifer Boothroyd.
        pages cm. — (Lightning bolt books. Healthy eating)
    Audience: Ages 5–8.
    Audience: K to grade 3.
    Includes bibliographical references and index.
    ISBN 978-1-4677-9471-8 (lb : alk. paper) — ISBN 978-1-4677-9673-6 (pb : alk. paper) —
ISBN 978-1-4677-9674-3 (eb pdf)
    1. Vegetarianism—Juvenile literature. I. Title.
TX392.B625 2016
613.2'6—dc23   2015015204

Manufactured in the United States of America
1 – BP – 12/31/15

Table of Contents

Food Choices

Look at all these choices! There are many reasons people choose the foods they eat.

People choose foods that taste good to them.

You and your friends may not like the same foods.

People choose foods that keep them healthy.

This girl helps make a healthy lunch.

Some families follow special diets because of their religion.

People choose foods because of their beliefs.

There are names to describe special diets people choose. Some of these names may be familiar to you. Others may be brand new.

Have you seen a label like this on foods? A gluten-free diet does not include a protein called gluten.

Vegetarian Diet

Have you heard of a vegetarian diet? These diets don't include meat.

This family eats a vegetarian diet.

Some vegetarians enjoy black bean burgers.

Vegetarians don't eat any meat at all, including chicken, fish, and turkey.

Vegetarians do eat some foods from animals.
They eat eggs.
They drink milk.

Most vegetarians eat lots of vegetables, fruits, and grains. These foods come from plants.

Eating a variety of veggies and fruits is good for you.

Vegetarians need to make sure they get iron. This nutrient is in beans and some grains.

Iron is added to some cereals.

Vegan Diet

Vegans don't eat meat or eggs. They don't drink milk from animals either.

Milk made from soy, nuts, or rice is a popular choice for vegans.

Vegans don't eat any foods that come from animals.

Vegans check ingredients to make sure that foods are vegan.

Eggs have protein.

Foods that come from animals are often rich in protein. So vegans must make sure to eat other foods with protein.

Vegans can get protein from plants. Beans and tofu have lots of protein.

Tofu is a soft, silky food made from soybeans.

Vegans also must make sure they get enough vitamin B12.

Vitamin B12 is often found in cheese, which is not a part of vegan diets.

Vegans need to eat foods with B12 added.

Some vegans take B12 vitamin pills to get the nutrients they need.

Calcium is another nutrient vegans must make sure to get. It is in milk and cheese. Vegans can get calcium from foods like kale and broccoli.

Kale is a kind of cabbage. Kale is in some salads.

Other Special Diets

Some people follow other special diets.

This family chooses foods that fit their diet.

They may not eat foods with added sugar.

No sugar has been added to this peanut butter.

They may eat only organic foods. These foods are grown without chemicals.

They may avoid gluten.
Gluten is in most breads.

Some bread is gluten-free.

They may eat only raw foods.

Many raw veggies are crunchy.

Some Jewish families eat a kosher diet. These diets follow certain rules, such as avoiding pork. Some Muslim families eat a halal diet. These diets also have special rules.

This store sells only halal foods.

All of these diets can be very healthy. **Just remember to get all the nutrients you need.**

Nutrients give you energy to play!

Try This!

This trail mix is good for people who don't eat gluten or added sugar. It is also good for vegans or vegetarians. But anyone can enjoy it! Ask an adult before you make it. And always wash your hands before touching food.

Ingredients

- sunflower seeds

- dried cranberries

- dried apple slices

- banana chips

- cashews

1. Put a handful of each ingredient into a resealable bag.

2. Close the bag and shake it.

3. Your trail mix is ready to eat!

Fun Facts

- Some people eat fish but no other meat. They are called pescatarians.

- Organic farmers don't use chemicals to keep bugs away. Instead, they use other bugs! They put these bugs on their crops to eat the bugs that eat their crops.

- Many foods are labeled for those who follow special diets. Next time you're in a grocery store, see if you can spot foods that are vegan, kosher, or gluten-free.

Glossary

calcium: a mineral that helps bones and teeth

diet: the foods and drinks you usually consume

nutrient: something needed by plants and animals to live and grow

protein: a substance in meat and some plants

raw: uncooked

vegan: a diet that does not include foods from animals, or a person who eats such a diet

vegetarian: a diet that does not include meat, or a person who eats such a diet

Further Reading

Ansh, Tamar. *Let My Children Cook! A Passover Cookbook for Kids.* Brooklyn: Judaica, 2014.

Bellisario, Gina. *Choose Good Food! My Eating Tips.* Minneapolis: Millbrook Press, 2014.

Choose MyPlate
http://www.choosemyplate.gov

Johnson, Kristi. *Grilled Pizza Sandwich and Other Vegetarian Recipes.* Mankato, MN: Capstone, 2009.

Kreisman, Rachelle. *You Want Me to Eat That? A Kids' Guide to Eating Right.* South Egremont, MA: Red Chair, 2015.

What's a Vegetarian?
http://kidshealth.org/kid/stay_healthy/food/vegetarian.html

Index

Photo Acknowledgments

The images in this book are used with the permission of: © iStockphoto.com/bhofack2, p. 2; © iStockphoto.com/luoman, p. 4; © Comstock Images/Getty Images, p. 5; © Dragon Images /Shutterstock.com, p. 6; Eye Ubiquitous/Newscom, p. 7; © Kevin Britland/Alamy, p. 8; © J.P. Nodier/Getty Images, p. 9; © Stocksign/CORBIS, p. 10; © Jamie Grill/JGI/Getty Images, p. 11; © Chamille White/Shutterstock.com, p. 12; © XinXinXing/Getty Images, p. 13; © Ilene MacdDonald/Alamy, p. 14; © Noel Hendrickson/Blend Images/Getty Images, p. 15; © Mieke Dalle/Getty Images, p. 16; © Michael Powell/Getty Images, p. 17; © MaraZe/Shutterstock.com, p. 18; © Boissonnet/BSIP/CORBIS, p. 19; © iStockphoto.com/Ehaurylik, p. 20; © Andersen Ross/Getty Images, p. 21; © studiomode/Alamy, p. 22; © Blend Images/Alamy, p. 23; © Rafael Ben-Ari/Alamy, p. 24; © Tetra Images/Getty Images, p. 25; © Kumar Sriskandan/Alamy, p. 26; © iStockphoto.com/MachineHeadz, p. 27; © Olaf Simon/Getty Images, p. 28.

Front cover: © bonchan/Shutterstock.com.

Main body text set in Johann Light 30/36.